Hognose Snakes

A Pet Care Guide for Hognose Snakes

Hognose Snakes General Info, Purchasing, Care, Cost, Keeping, Health, Supplies, Food, Breeding and More Included!

By Lolly Brown

Copyrights and Trademarks

Disclaimer and Legal Notice

Foreword

Hognose snakes can really be a great pet for new keepers or even for people who doesn't have any experience on handling snakes. They really have a low disposition which is a great factor since aggression is not a problem. They are very passive and grow into a manageable size. If you are planning to buy this kind of pet, you must make sure that you are well-informed with its biological information, temperament, and needs. You must make sure that you are capable of handling it properly and that you are physically, emotionally, and financially ready in order to become a responsible snake owner.

We got you covered! With the help of this book you'll be able to learn all the necessary information you need to know about Hognose snakes from its heritage, maintenance, health, down to its specific needs with regards to habitat, nutrition, breeding, and licensing as well. We hope that this book will be of great help for you whether you are an expert or a newbie when it comes to Hognose snakes. Enjoy!

Table of Contents

Introduction

Hognose snakes are harmless nonvenomous snakes. They are distinguished by their distinctive upturned stout. Their original range is in North America, Madagascar, and South America. They are considered "diurnal" which means the time they are most active is during the day. In general, Hognose snakes attain the length of 12 inches to 40 inches depending on what specie it belongs to. Their color and pattern varies but their predominant shade is blotches of light brown with a beige-colored background. They are very timid and become frantic whenever threatened. They have the ability to make an impression of a dead body intensified with a foul smell they can produce.

Hognose Snakes are unlikely to be hostile making them easy to be managed. They might strike with their mouths closed or they might even play dead. Although they are part of the wild, their aggression is at the lowest level. It is need of on-going care and maintenance as it is a component for their welfare.

In the following chapters, you'll gain knowledge on the basics of Hognose snake care like its general information, temperament and its biological background. You'll also learn how to provide their needs and take care of them with regard to maintenance, nutrition, health, habitat, and breeding. Through this you will be able to see if a Hognose snake is an ideal pet for you.

Snakes, in general, can look scary and surely is not for the faint of heart but through this book you'll be able to realize that this reptile can become a great pet for you and your family.

Chapter One: Biological Information

If you are planning to have a Hognose snake as your pet, you should make sure that you are really capable of handling such reptile. Owning a snake might look appealing and challenging. Although you have a heart for this creature, it doesn't mean that you are suit to have one as a pet. You must first be able to understand how their nature works and see to it if you'll be able to handle them.

Through this chapter the general information and biological facts of Hognose snakes will be given. You'll also gain knowledge about its sub-species in order for you to determine what kind of Hognose snake would best suit you and your family. Remember that you must be certain that you have the will and the capacity to be a snake owner as it is a very huge responsibility.

Taxonomy, Origin and Distribution

Hognose Snakes have a scientific name of Heterodon nasicus/ simus/ platyrhinos .They belong in Kingdom *Animalia*, Phylum *Chordata*, Class *Reptilia*, Order *Squamata*, Family *Dipsadidae*, Genus H*eterodon*, and Species nasicus/ simus/ platyrhinos.

Hognose snakes are harmless nonvenomous snakes. Their range is originally situated in North America, Madagascar, and South America They are often avoided and considered as blow snakes or puff adders.

The name "Hognose" was derived from their distinctive upturned stout which has the capacity to dig on loose sand or soil using a side to side or sweeping motion in order to find food or escape whenever there is a need to do so. They also tend to burrow in humus.

They are considered "diurnal" which means the time they are most active is during daytime. They are usually situated in areas that are dry and sandy.

Size, Life Span, and Physical Appearance

In general, Hognose snakes attain the length of 12 inches to 40 inches depending on the specie it belongs to. Their color and pattern varies extremely but their predominant shade is blotches of light brown with a beige-colored background. They also come in red, brown, orange, black with markings, green, yellow with black checkerboard patterns, tan, and they tend to have a tricolour as well in the mix of white, red, and black.

They are rear-fanged and possess mild venom which they use in order to prepare themselves in swallowing their prey - usually toads - whole. Whenever they are threatened, they flatten their head and neck followed by a strike with a loud hiss. They are known for their defensive plays like the ones mentioned but they usually have a low disposition and rarely bite. In general, they get easily accustomed on the new environment and circumstances they face after being captured.

They can live an average life of 15 years but some can reach until 18 years depending on the care being provided.

Sub – Species of Hognose Snakes

There are three species of Hognose snakes. Read carefully and find out which type of hognose snake will suit you best.

Heterodon Nasicus - Western Hognose

Distribution: Southern Canada, Arizona, Northern Mexico, New Mexico, and Texas

Physical characteristics:

Length: 24 inches to 84 inches

Body: Its stout body is covered with keeled scales and it has a sharply upturned snout. Its ground color comes in a variety ranging from brown, gray or olive, tan, and somewhat has dark blotches with a square or bar shape that runs along its body longitudinally. It has black scales that are glossy. Its scales can often be white, orange, or yellow.

Behavior and Nature: Western Hognose is known for its defensive plays which includes a loud hiss by forcing the air through its skull and rostral bone structure. If threatened, it has the capacity to flatten its body that might be an attempt to make itself look dangerous and larger that would sent the predator away. It might also strike but usually with a closed mouth either forward or sideways to knock its predator down with the use of its keeled snout without the need of biting. It is also known for being able to play dead whenever it's tired defending itself.

Heterodon Platyrhinos- Eastern Hognose

Distribution: Florida, New England, Great Lakes Region, Southern Canada, Georgia, South Carolina.

Physical characteristics:

Length: 28 inches to 46 inches

Body: They are distinguished by their distinctive upturned stout. Their body background can be gray, black, brown, yellow, green. It has rectangular spots in the middle of its back and has keeled scales. The females have a fine taper to the end of its tails. On the other hand, males have a bulge near the tail and cloaca then obviously tapers off.

Behavior and Nature: Eastern Hognose snakes are very much active during the day and they can often be seen on the roads during fall and spring. They are very timid and become frantic whenever threatened. They have the ability to make an impression of a dead body intensified with a foul smell they can produce.

Heteredon Simus- Southern Hognose Snake

Distribution: South Carolina, North Carolina, Florida, Georgia

Physical characteristics:

Length: 14 inches to 24 inches

Body: Southern Hognose Snakes come in colors tan, gray, or reddish with a hint of dark brown blotches at the center of its back and along the sides. The underside of their tails is the same color with their belly. They have a sharper upturned snout.

Behavior and Nature: Southern Hognose snakes are less elaborate compared to the Eastern Hognose snake but still, they display hissing, neck spreading, and playing dead whenever under threat.

Quick Facts

Distribution and Range: North America, Madagascar, South America

Breed Size: long and large – size breed

Body Type and Appearance: Has big eyes with rounded pupils with a large head but narrow necks. Usually have dark stripes on top of its head

Length: length of 12 inches to 40 inches depending on what specie it belongs

Skin Texture: scaly or has keeled scales

Color: Their color and pattern varies extremely but their predominant shade is blotches of light brown with a beige-colored background.

Temperament: non – venomous; known for their defensive plays like hissing and playing dead but they usually have a low disposition and rarely bite

Diet: toads, rodents, lizards, salamanders, invertebrates, small mammals

Habitat: Areas that are dry and sandy

Health Conditions: generally healthy but can be sick from the common illness like Parasites (External and Internal), Dehydration, Dysecdysis, Vomiting and Regurgitation, Infectious Stomatitis (Mouth Rot), and Pneumonia.

Lifespan: They can live an average life of 15 years but some can reach until 18 years depending on the care being provided.

Chapter Two: Hognose Snakes as Pets

After being able to know the basic facts about Hognose snakes as well as its sub species, brace yourself for there is still tons of information you have to be knowledgeable about in order to be sure that this powerful reptile is meant to become your pet.

In this chapter, you'll be able to see how Hognose snakes behave as a pet more specifically its temperament. We'll give you pointers as well with regard to the licensing of snakes along with the requirements you need to bring in order to do so. Plus we'll give you an overview on how much money you'll need in order to keep one. Remember that it is your responsibility as an owner to keep your pet happy, safe, and satisfied. Therefore, being physically, emotionally, and financially ready is a must.

What Makes It a Great Pet

Being able to get along with your pet is very vital in order to build a strong relationship with it. As we all know, this is a long-term commitment so you should be very certain that you and the pet you have chosen will enjoy each other's company. Knowing the temperament as well as other characteristics of a Hognose snake is very important as it is the way for you see if both of your qualities match well.

Temperament and Behavioral Characteristics with other Pets

Although they came from the same kind, snakes do differ in terms of behavior or temperament. In this segment you'll learn how Hognose snakes deal with its owner, how its nature works, and how do they interact with other people and other pets as well. Hognose Snakes are unlikely to be hostile making them easy to be managed. Although they are part of the wild, their aggression is at the lowest level. Snakes often bite but not Hognose Snakes. They rarely try to bite owners as even in the most threatened circumstance. They might strike with their mouths closed or they might even play dead. They get easily accustomed to the new environment they belong to. Their low disposition can be maintained especially if they are properly socialized.

They are very active during day time and they are very curious about their surroundings. They can actually find smallest of holes making escape easier and so you must really pay attention on its housing requirements which will be further discussed on the next chapters. It is need of on-going care and maintenance as it is a component for their welfare. But don't worry because it only needs the basic kind of care.

If you are living with your family, this kind of snake can help them overcome their curiosity about it. You can actually let them handle it as they are docile and calm over time. There's no need for you to worry about your pet causing trouble. If domesticated properly, they will be the friendliest reptile you have met.

Their temperament toward other pets is just the same unless they are toads and rodents since these two are their main prey. They can get along well with other animals as long as they have been properly socialized with each other. But it is still best not to associate them with other animals.

Pros and Cons of Hognose Snakes

It is a common instinct that when you heard the word "snake" you'll be able to associate it with the word "venom " or "poison" but did you know that not all snakes are poisonous for humans? Great examples are Hognose snakes. This probably is the major pro for this kind of pet. The venom that they have inside their body are only used for the process of swallowing their prey whole. They are unlikely to use biting as a defense mechanism. Instead, they rely on bluffing ploys like playing dead in order to escape extreme situations. When they are threatened, they may strike but with their mouths closed. They really have a low disposition which is a great factor since aggression is not a problem. They are very passive and grow into a manageable size. This can really be a great pet for new keepers and young people who don't have any experience on handling snakes.

Having said all its positive side, let's now move on its counterpart, the negative one. This pet is definitely not for those who have a faint heart as living with a snake can really make you feel unusual unless you are strong-willed to really keep one. It cannot also be trained though it can be socialized. You cannot expect so much from this pet, unlike dogs who can express what their feel through their body language. The food it needs might only be purchased on pet shops or reptile stores. They can live for 15 years which is a downside as it may be hard to rehome.

If you are a snake lover, you must consider that not everyone you know would be fond of the same thing. If you are living with your family or roommates, it might be a challenge on how you'll be able to pursue or even convince them to live with a snake but don't worry for there are ways to make it possible. It might take some time but remember that patience is a virtue!

Here are the following tips on how you'll be able to win over their hearts for a Hognose Snake.

- **Know the snake you are about to purchase.** Before anything else, you must first know the specie you are interested in. You should gather all the information you need in order to be well educated with regard to the pet you want to have. You should be able to answer generic questions like how much will it cost, how big will it get, what kind of food does it eat, what kind of care does it require, etc. So that if ever your family ask about these questions, you'll be knowledgeable enough to answer it with confidence. Giving them the right answers can help them see how eager and willing you are to own a Hognose snake.

- **Break it to them gently.** Everything takes time and you shouldn't rush things. Do not immediately drop the news that you want a snake as a pet especially if the members of your family are uptight with this idea. Instead, you can give them hints that you are being fond of snakes lately. You can tell them stories about the snake owners you know and their experiences in taking care of a snake. By this way, they'll know that it isn't really that hard to maintain a snake and they might even be an ideal pet for the family.

- **Do not force them to agree with you instantly.** It is very unlikely that your family members or roommates will accept the idea overnight. If ever they still stand against it do not be angry or feel frustrated. It might take weeks, months, or even years. Just be patient encouraging them in the best possible way you can. Just be calm and do your best in persuading them. You'll surely win their favor when you talk it to them constantly.

- **Assure them that you are going to be a responsible owner.** If ever your roommate or family saw how willing and able you are to take care of a snake, this can be a great factor in order to make them say yes with it. Show them that you will be able to commit yourself with your potential pet and that you will be responsible enough to provide it with their needs.

- **Respect the decision of your housemates. Wait until they approve with having a snake at home.** No matter how much you like having a snake as your pet you must still consider your housemates' decision. If they do not really approve, wait until they do so. You must respect their feelings towards it as it is not only you who's going to deal with the snake but they will too. In that case, it is better for you not to buy at all. If you disregard their opinion about it, it may just cause you a problem. It might be the root of misunderstanding. You may be forced to re-locate your pet or bring it shelters and have it for adoption.

Snake Licensing

Licensing a Hognose Snake

Hognose Snakes need not to be licensed since they are categorized as non-venomous meaning that even if their bite won't kill anyone as the venom they have won't harm human unless they are allergic to it. But still it depends on which state or country you belong. There might not be a mandatory requirement for licensing but permits might be regulated. Make sure that you are familiar with all the laws or ordinance in the place you live in with regard to snake licensing.

Although it is not mandatory to have your Hognose snake licensed you may still need to have a permit for the sake of your snake's safety. If ever your pet will slip away there and someone found it, there might be a need for you to present your license/permit in order to prove that you are the owner and you are keeping your snake legally. If you are not able to present such, you might pay charges or worse, your pet might not be returned to you. There are also veterinarians that ask for a permit before they attend to your snake's medical needs. They want to make sure that you are keeping such pet legally before anything else.

Necessary documents needed

- Owner's identification documents

- Pet Insurance

- Medical History

- Micro-chipping

- Medical Certificates

- Other proofs showing that you have bought your snake from a recognized breeder who breed them in captivity and not just caught in the wild.

These are just documents that are generally required by states, regions, or towns but it may vary. It is recommended for you to inquire on the nearest licensing office in your location in order to be certain on the documents you have to prepare. Make sure you have the complete requirements in order to have it processed immediately. Some places may ban having reptiles as pets so make sure that you can legally have them.

Traveling with your snake pet

If you are planning to travel with your pet snake, there will surely be a regulation about this matter. License and/ or permits will be very necessary in exporting, importing, or even traveling with naturally dangerous and exotic animals. There might be special laws that you have to abide with depending on which country, state, or region you are planning to visit. You should make a thorough research on bringing your pet to other places on which you will stay. Be sure to check the rules on the airlines you're flying with or the ship you are getting aboard. Be knowledgeable about these things to avoid problems in your future travels.

Cost of Owning a Snake

Generally, having a pet regardless if it's a high or low maintenance one can be costly. In order to own and take care of a snake, you must also be financially ready as the supplies it will need will surely add up to your expenses. Through this section, you'll be given an overview of the expenses you might have to manage in order to keep and purchase a snake. Supplies for maintenance, food, enclosures or its habitat, veterinary care, and other on-going essential costs that you have to cover and make sure that you budget is enough for these costs.

The cost will vary depending on where you have purchased the supplies, the nutrient content of the food you are going to provide, the size and quality of the enclosure, the time being, the kind of equipment your snake needs, etc. All these expenses might be quite overwhelming and so you must really prepare yourself and your wallet as well for you to be able to attend all the costs it entails. The cost of the snake itself, accessories, substrate, initial medical check-ups, licensing, micro-chipping, equipment, and food are just some of the expenses you have to initially cover. Stay tuned, for we'll help you know more of these pet related expenses.

- **Hognose Snake: $50- $100**

    The price of a Hognose snake ranges from $50- $100 but this may depend on the age of the snake and on the pricing of the breeder as well. If the Hognose snake is being sold at a very low price, and if it seems suspicious do not transact with the breeder. Make sure that you are going purchase a high-quality snake from a reputable breeder.

- **Housing**

Enclosure ($80- $100) *this may vary depending on size*

    Hognose snakes are exceptional escape artists so make sure that they will not find even a slightest opportunity to escape. Make sure that the enclosure you are going to put your snake in is well fastened and tight. Baby or hatchling snakes can stay inside a 12 x 6 inch enclosure until they reach one year old. On the other hand, an adult hognose snake can stay inside a 20-gallon sized cage. You can also use standard fish tanks as an enclosure, just make sure that it has screen cover. Set up the enclosure whether you are maintaining multiple cages for several snakes or if for an individual snake only. You can fix the habitat you are preparing to make it pleasing and homey.

Substrate ($10- $15)

A substrate will act as the bedding for the enclosure you have prepared. Avoid using cedar as it is toxic to reptiles as well as sand or gravel since they are non-absorbent and they may promote bacterial growth which can infect your pet snake. You could use paper towels, newspaper, pine shavings, or aspen.

Hiding ($5- $10)

This kind of snake needs his own hiding place in order to make them feel secure as this is what they do in the wild. The spot on where they can hide can be made out of plastic or rock caves that you can purchase on local pet stores. You can improvise by using small box with a hole for their access. Their hiding spot should be large enough for them to fit in. It is recommended that you provide two hide spots inside its cage; on both the unheated and heated side.

Heating ($5 above)

The health of your pet should not be compromised. You must be able to provide the equipment to keep your snake healthy. 75- 85 degree Fahrenheit is the ideal temperature for a Hognose snake. You must install a heat pad or heat tape covering 1/3 of the surface of the cage.

- **Food**

Separate food tank ($30- $60)

You can use a separate tank in order to store the food you have for your snake. In this way the habitat would not be used during feeding time.

Food ($10 - $20) *price may vary according to the brand*

Toads are what Hognose snakes eat in the wild but you may insist on feeding them with mice. You may purchase rodents or other species on a pet store. You can buy online but be mindful that there might be a shipping fee allocated with your order. Try to buy in bulk for it will help you save more.

- **Veterinary Care/ Medical Care** ($75- $100)

It is advisable for your pet to visit the vet once in a while for a routine check-up in order to make sure that its health is exceptional. You should also set aside a budget in case of emergency like if it has bitten someone, though it's non-venomous and rarely happens but still this kind of circumstance is in need of medical care.

- **Licensing/ Permit/ Micro-chipping** ($20 -$100 and more)

The amount you pay for these may vary depending on the state, region, or country on which you belong.

Chapter Three: Purchasing and Selecting a Healthy Breed

After being able to know how a Hognose snake behaves as a pet as well as its need in terms of food, housing, licensing, etc., it's now time for you to be able to choose a healthy breed. If you really think that this specie is an ideal pet for you, you must be able to select and purchase a healthy Hognose snake from a highly-regarded and trustworthy breeder legally.

In this chapter, we'll give some criteria you should consider in choosing a Hognose snake as well as the points you should be mindful about in order to determine whether the breeder you are dealing with is reputable or not. Links on where you can purchase a Hognose snake online will be provided at the latter part of this chapter. Being able to purchase a healthy breed is the first step towards a happy life with your pet.

Where to Purchase an Hognose Snake Breed

This section will discuss the different places where you can purchase your own Hognose snake along with its pros and cons as well as some tips on how to avoid bad or illegal snake breeders.

Reptile Shops

It is highly advisable that you purchase a Hognose snake on the nearest reptile shop in your place. Even the novice and expert snake keepers, veterinarians, and reptile enthusiast recommend it.

Pros

The best thing about buying on reptile shops is that you'll be able to ask questions about your chosen breed to the staff attending to your needs as they are experts with species of various breeds. In here, you can find various types of snakes even those that are not available on your local pet stores which give you more option.

Cons

The price is usually fix and you cannot negotiate with it which can be a problem for those who already budget their money for a specific amount

Private Breeders

Private breeders are the ones who are raising and taking care of Hognose snakes first-hand. Their character may mirror the kind of snakes they breed. For example if they look responsible enough, it means that the snakes in his custody are being well taken care of.

Pros

The prices are negotiable. This is recommended for those who want to be practical about price. Another good thing about purchasing from private breeders is that you can ask for tips on how to take care of your pet as they are the ones who personally know their characteristics. If the breeder asks information about yourself it means that he is making sure that the snake you have chosen will be at the right hands at it also means that he is a trustworthy breeder.

Cons

Finding a reputable private breeder can be tricky. Sometimes they may seem of high repute but the truth is they aren't really taking care of the snakes well so you must be very careful.

Reptile Shows

Reptile shows are events being held for all the reptile enthusiasts. This is something you might enjoy.

Pros

The price of snakes here are a lot cheaper than any pet shops or private breeders. In here, you'll be able to meet snake owners and you can actually ask them to whom, of all the breeders found in the show, should you buy because definitely they are a patron on this kind of event.

Cons

Reptile shows aren't an annual thing and might not be available at you are at the very moment. This might be a problem if you badly want to own a pet snake immediately.

Rescue Centers

If you want a pet snake but would like to skip the part of raising them for a long time, you are a season keeper. If that's the case, you might want to try having a snake from rescue centers. There are lots of pets being abandoned and rescue centers are the ones giving them shelter until their new owner comes.

Pros

You may get species here for free or for a minimal amount only. All you have to do is to prove that you are responsible enough in taking care of them. If you acquire a snake from here, you are actually saving their lives and giving them a fresh start and a new hope.

Cons

The availability of the different species of Hognose snakes might be limited and you may not have many options to choose from or you may have no options at all.

How to Spot a Good Snake Breeder

After gaining knowledge on where you can buy a Hognose snake, it's now time to determine who to buy it from. Being able to transact with a breeder who's caring, reputable, and responsible is something you should make sure of. To give you an idea on what should a reputable breeder be. Here are the following pointers you should need to look at in order to choose a reputable snake breeder:

- They should be knowledgeable enough about the breed/ specie of snake they are raising. They must be able to provide you information on how this breed behave and how it should properly be taken care of

- Their main reason for breeding a snake should not be because of the money or business and not because it is their hobby but for the primary purpose of keeping it healthy.

- They should be able to guide you on how to set up the enclosure properly, where you should put it, and what level of humidity/ temperature does the snake need for its habitat.

- They should be able to provide you other information that isn't typical. They should know more than a pet store clerk. If they only provide you with details that are general, there's a big chance that they aren't really pet enthusiasts.

- Reputable breeders should be able to build a good relationship with their potential/ existing buyers as they are like handing you their pet as well knowing that they are the ones who have taken care of them in the first place. You may ask from their previous buyers referrals in order for you to know more about this breeder you are dealing with and if they can be trusted.

- If the breeder loves and keeps on telling stories and information about the animals they are breeding, it means that they really do love pets. Whenever you ask them questions, they should look happily answer all your inquiries. If from the start they are starting to ignore you, there's a big chance that they will also be as unresponsive as they are after you have spent your money or when the sale has been done.

- Good Breeders have lots of patience especially to those who keep on asking questions. They have the initiative to share what they know without getting frustrated or angry with them.

- They should ask questions about you as they are making sure that you are responsible enough to handle whichever pet you have chosen. This is actually a good sign that the breeder care about pets.

Some Questions You Can Ask to Spot a Good Breeder

- Information about Hognose snakes and the sub-species it has and how do they differ
- The habitat it must dwell in
- The kind of enclosure it needs
- The kind of food the snake eats
- Brand of foods recommended for snakes
- The way the breeder raised and breed the snakes
- The diet of the snakes as to the frequency of its feeding time
- The right temperature for it
- The breeder's experiences on raising a snake
- Personal information of the breeder like his specialization and the reason why he chose to become a snake breeder
- The number of years the breeder has been in the industry
- The warranty or guarantee it offers as well as its duration
- Referrals

Characteristics of a Healthy Breed

Whether you choose a baby Hognose, juvenile or an adult, there are several things to keep in mind when selecting a healthy breed.

Eye: It should be free from any sign of discharge or cloudiness. It should be clear unless of course if the snake is beginning to shed its skin.

Breathing: Make sure that the snake is healthy breathing and that there are no signs of discharge in the nostrils and that it's free from any signs of labor breathing

Body: The body of the snake should be rounded without any injuries. If the snake has a smooth and supple skin or if has blisters do not purchase it as these are signs of ill health. It should also have no mobility issues and should have the capacity to move freely. If the snake has raised scale avoid purchasing it as might be infected with motes. There should be no discharge found in the anus and the ventral opening should be easily distinguished from the underside. It should use its tongue in order to inspect its environment and whenever you lift it up there should be a sense of strength that you should feel in its body

Type: Choosing a Hognose snake that is bred in captivity is highly recommended since the snakes coming from the wild might be infected with ailments and parasite, they might be a little hard to handle since they aren't socialized well, and their background might not be good as they aren't raised or have been domesticated.

List of Breeders and Rescue Websites

Buying or even looking for a pet online can be really convenient. Within just one click you'll be able to look into the available species each breeder sells. However, there still a need for you to personally check and pick up the pet you have chosen.

You must be really careful in dealing with breeders online since other sites might deceive you. In order to make sure that you are visiting a good website checks if it has complete contact information. If the site looks suspicious do not take any risk and fin another one. In order to help you make sure that you are on the right track we have here below a list of breeders and adoption rescue websites in the United States and in the United Kingdom.

United States Breeders and Rescue Websites

Geckos Etc.

<http://www.geckosetc.com/available_hognose.html>

Kingsnake.com

<http://market.kingsnake.com/index.php?cat=97>

Superconda

<http://www.superconda.com/>

South Texas Dragons. com

<https://www.southtexasdragons.com/western-hognose.html>

Undergound Reptiles

<https://undergroundreptiles.com/product-category/animals/snakes/hognose-snakes/>

Snakes at Sunset

<http://snakesatsunset.com/snakes-for-sale/>

Cutting Edge Herp

<http://www.cuttingedgeherp.com/westernhognosesnakes.html>

Agriseek

<http://www.agriseek.com/market/p/Baby-Eastern-Hognose.htm>

XYZ Reptiles

<https://www.xyzreptiles.com/>

Dino Reptiles

<https://www.dinoreptiles.com/>

Everything Reptile

<http://www.everythingreptile.org/western-hognose-snake.html>

E and J Reptile Shows & Rescue

<http://www.eandjreptileshows.com/>

JB's Rattles

<http://www.jbsrattles.com/www.jbsrattles.com/Reptile_Rescue.html>

Southeastern Reptile Rescue

<http://www.snakesareus.com/our_western_hognoses>

Forgotten Friend Reptile Sanctuary

<https://forgottenfriend.org/>

Snake Rescue NJ

<http://snakes-n-scales.com/snake-rescue-nj/>

United Kingdom Breeders and Rescue Websites

Crag Top Hognose

<http://www.cragtophognose.co.uk/>

Gumtree

<https://www.gumtree.com/reptiles/england/hognose/>

Hognose Snakes

<http://www.hognose.co.uk/>

NewsNow UK

<https://www.newsnow.co.uk/classifieds/pets-animals/hognose-snake-for-sale-uk.html>

Hogmorphs

<http://hogmorphs.co.uk/>

UK Exotics

<http://hogmorphs.co.uk/>

Little Snakes

<http://littlesnakes.co.uk/>

Reptile Cymru

<http://www.reptilecymru.co.uk/>

The Reptile Room

<https://thereptileroom.co.uk/>

Exotic Pets

<https://www.exotic-pets.co.uk/snakes-for-sale.html>

Reptilia Reptile Rescue

<http://reptiliareptilerescue.co.uk/>

Snake Busters

<http://www.snakebusters.com/>

North East Reptile Rescue

<http://nerr.co.uk/>

RSCPA Reptile Rescue

<http://www.rspcareptilerescue.co.uk/>

Proteus Reptile Trust Rescue

<http://www.proteusreptiletrust.org/>

North East Reptile Rescue

<http://nerr.co.uk/>

Chapter Four: Habitat Requirements for Hognose Snakes

The environment your snake is living in is a vital factor contributing to its well-being. Although it may seem complicated, setting up an enclosure or a cage for your Hognose snake is not really that hard. All you have to do is to make sure that you have all the necessary materials needed as well as how and where to put those things on its proper place. In this chapter, we'll help you hand in hand in preparing a home for your pet snake. We'll give you a list of all the paraphernalia needed along with its function. We'll also give you some tips on how to clean and keep your pet's enclosure away from any bacterial growth.

Steps on How to Set Up Your Snake's Enclosure

Step 1: Find the right size tank

The major item that should be in your list is a 20-gallon tank for your Hognose Snake. It is the recommended size for a regular-sized snake but you may buy a bigger cage if ever it's too small for an adult snake. In order for you to help your snake adjust easily from the new environment it lives in, you must make its new home somehow similar to the wild it naturally belongs too. This part can be exciting as you are going to build a safe and personal space of your pet. Make sure that you will have the patience and the creativity as well to ensure that you'll be providing it with an enclosure it's going to love.

Step 2: Decide where you are going to place the heating paraphernalia

The next thing you have to do is to determine where you are going to set up the heating equipment for the enclosure. You must decide where to put the heating pads as you need to provide a normal and hot side for your pet. You should be able to assign a specific location for a basking area as well as an area with a normal temperature on where your pet can coil up and rest. After being able to determine such, you'll be able to know where all the other materials should be located properly.

Step 3: Add the substrate/ bedding of your choice

The third one is the substrate or bedding of the enclosure. Be sure that you are using snake-friendly materials for there are some that might potentially harm your pet. Avoid using cedar as this material is toxic to reptiles and we recommend that you stay away from using gravel or sand since these are non-absorbent which may cause bacterial growth that may infect and make your pet ill. It is advisable that you use aspen as the primary material for the substrate as it provides a nice thick layer of bedding. Hognose snakes love to burrow so expect that they'll be staying at the bottom of the cage you have set up. By this way they will feel safe and secured.

Aspen bedding is very easy to clean and it will help you maintain the cleanliness of the whole enclosure. It has the capacity to hold the moisture well which can be a helping factor whenever the snake is shedding since moisture level can rise during the process. Also you can use simple things for the bedding like paper towels, pine shavings, and newspapers.

Step 4: Add the necessary accessories inside the cage

The next step in line that you have to do is to be able to place all the materials like the water dish, food bowl, perches, some nice plants, and your snake's hiding spot inside the cage. Make sure that the size of these materials is appropriate for the age of your snake. To make the cage more appealing to the eyes, you can add up bamboo bars on which your snake may perch along with jungle vines of which it may climb upon. You can add up any accessories you like just sure that you will not overdo it as your pet needs a space to roam around in its enclosure. All you need here is a strong imagination and your creativity in order to create a whole new world for your pet snake.

The hiding spot that your snake needs can be purchased on local pet stores. Make sure that the size of it matches well with that of your snake. It comes in a variety of style and colors. You may buy one that looks like crystal caves, habba huts, turtle shell, skull, and many more. You can decide whatever decor you may like as long as it won't be too big especially if it is for a baby snake.

Baby snakes tend to like being inside a small dark hiding place on which they find their comfort and security, they are fond of being contained and covered in all sides. They do not like being exposed too much so make sure that you are being mindful of these facts. You can also improvise by stacking branch, sticks, and cork flaps as these materials can make a nice bedding as well as a comfy hiding place. In order to create more effect, you can add mosses and leaves to its cage which replicates the surroundings it has in the wild.

Make sure that the snake will be able to use all the hiding spots, branches, or caves you have purchased. Do not just place it on top of the bedding. You must be able to bury it halfway through the substrate so there is no need for your snake to come out from the burrow for it to use these.

Step 5: Install all the heating equipment

After you have staged the whole enclosure, it's now time for you to set up the basking lamp, under tank heater, and the humidity and heat gauges.

Regulating Temperature

The ideal temperature for a Hognose snake ranges from 75- 85 degree Fahrenheit and this must strictly be regulated. The next section will inform you about the equipment you need to install in order to attain the ideal temperature.

Tank heater

You must be able to install a tank heater or heat pad on bottom of the cage under the spot that is provided for the basking area.

Overheat lamp/ basking lamp

Put the overheat lamp or basking lamp which looks like a UVB like on the top of the lid of the cage in order to warm up its sides especially during the cold season. If the season is not that cold, there is no need for you to light it up. You can put a dimmer on the lamp for you to be able to turn the light down a bit.

The basking area should only occupy 1/3 of the whole enclosure. Be mindful of the heat requirement of Hognose snakes. Make sure that it is being applied. Remember that you should not place water bowls in the basking area but instead put it on the cooler side of the cage.

Analog Temperature

In order to be sure that the cage has really attained the needed temperature, you may attach an analog thermometer close to the hiding spot or substrate of your pet snake. Make sure to regularly check temperatures especially when summer time comes and the whole place is warmer.

Chapter Five: Nutrition and Feeding

The health of your Hognose snake should never be compromised as it plays a great factor on its life expectancy as well as in its immunity against any sickness. You must make sure that your pet is being provided with the nutrition it needs. Usually, factors such as age, body, and level of activity are being considered in order to determine its nutritional diet needs.

Through this chapter, you'll be knowledgeable about your pet's needs when it comes to nutrition. There will be some guidelines given as to what food your snake should eat and how frequent should they be fed.

FAQs about the Nutritional Needs of Hognose Snakes

What should Hognose snakes eat?

In the wild, Hognose snakes being their carnivorous selves would feed on toads, birds, and lizards. But when they are already held captive the diet you'll be able to provide for them will of course be limited. The best food you can give them is domesticated rodents which are already frozen and easy to stock in your freezer, though there is still a need for you to warm it before serving it to your pet. You can warm it up by putting the frozen rodents you are going to serve in a sealed plastic and dip it into lukewarm water.

It is recommended for you to buy in big bulks in order for you to save money. Avoid feeding your Hognose snake with prey caught in the wild since it can transmit parasites and your snake might get used to it making it hard for you to provide them with that kind of food. Do not provide them live rodents as their food since it might only exhaust your pet from catching its prey.

Do Hognose snakes need other vitamins source like supplements?

There's no need for you to provide vitamin powder or supplements for your snake. They can already absorb all the vitamins and minerals they need from the food that you are serving so there's no need for you to add anything on their meal.

Should I let my Hognose snake catch its own prey?

Other snake owners keep on insisting that their snake needs the thrill of hunting through catching its own prey but this idea is actually not true. Live preys can be too active for your pet. If you let your snake catch a live prey there is a tendency that it might get hurt from the process and it could also result to exhaustion, being scarred and disfigured, and even frightened of it. Having said that, it is recommended that you feed your Hognose snake with a pre-killed prey as it is safer.

Where can I buy food for my snake?

There are many wholesale companies and private breeders who actually breed their own rodents that are intended to become a food for your Hognose snake. Usually, they sell bags of frozen rodents. Be sure to strive for the freshest stock of rodents available. Buy in bulk as it may help you save bucks.

Feeding Conditions

In order to encourage your snake to eat, you must make sure that nothing's going to bother it. During feeding time, your snake should be away from any factors that might cause them to lose their appetite. Below are some tips on how to improve the feeding conditions for your Hognose Snake.

Tip 1: Keep its habitat properly maintained

The environment your snake lives in is a factor affecting its appetite. Make sure that the habitat you have set up for your pet is properly maintained and complete with all the lighting, layout, accessories, humidity, and other requirements needed by your pet. If ever the enclosure you have prepared is not pleasing and cannot give enough comfort for your pet, it might lost its appetite or worse, it might even refuse the food you are serving.

Tip 2: Provide a separate tank for feeding

Just like humans, it is better for us to have a dining area on which we can enjoy our meals. This also goes for snakes. Though it is not required for you to have a separate tank intended for feeding your pet, this is something you should provide since it can be helpful in maintaining the enclosure of your pet clean and sanitized. Whenever you are going to put your snake on its feeding tank, it will be in his instinct that he will be fed making it easier for you to feed them.

Feeding Amount and Frequency

Hognose snakes have a high metabolism rate. They need to be fed a minimum of twice per week. The recommended size of a snake's meal should not be bigger than the width of the its body or the size of the meal should only leave a small lump in its body. Do not overfeed your snake during feeding time as they may spend most of their time and energy just to digest the food making them lazy plus it might cause them digestive problems. You may ask your breeder or your vet with regard to the amount of food you should provide your pet with.

Guidelines in Feeding Your Hognose Snake

- After feeding your Hognose snake, do not handle it for at least 24 hours. Let it digest the food first for it to absorb all the nutrients it needs. It is not ideal for you to handle them right away so avoid doing so.

- Make sure that your snakes have access to fresh water. Remember to check if the dish has enough water for your pet and constantly replenish them with it.

- Do not force them to eat when they refuse to. Give them some time. When they become hungry they will surely grab the food you have prepared.

- Though it is unlikely for Hognose snakes to bite, it is still advisable for you to use thongs in order to avoid accidental bites.

- Do not serve frozen pre-killed prey. Instead, place it inside a plastic bag and thaw it under running warm water. Make sure that it is warmer than the room temperature, by this way it will smell more appetizing to your snake.

Make sure that you are able to feed your pet with the correct size of meal they need. As they grow older, the size of their meal should be adjusted.

Chapter Six: Maintenance for Hognose Snakes

Providing an environment which somehow replicates the wilderness for your snake is a great start for them to really feel at home but it doesn't stop there. As an owner, you must make sure that you are able to maintain a clean and sanitized place for your snake in order for it to live a happy and healthy life. Providing them with all their needs from food down to a nice place to burrow would surely heighten the quality of life your snake has.

In this chapter we'll give you some tips on how to keep your snake's enclosure squeaky clean and free from bacteria. You'll also be given some points on how you'll be able to make your home a snake-friendly one.

Spot Cleaning Your Snake's Enclosure

What is spot cleaning?

Spot cleaning doesn't only intend cleaning the enclosure but it goes for all the materials placed inside the cage as well. It is your responsibility to maintain the cleanliness of your pet's cage. The enclosure can become a ground for bacterial growth caused by the humidity level inside it. It is recommended that you regularly clean it as reptiles are prone to bacterial and skin infection and an unclean surrounding might trigger it.

Make sure that each area of the cage has been properly sanitized as well as all the accessories inside it like the water bowl which should be disposed and replaced more than once a week in order to prevent bacteria accumulation. See to it that the fecal matter of your snake will be removed immediately as well as their shed skin and left over food.

How often should I clean my pet's enclosure?

It is recommended that you clean your snake's cage at least once a day, or every other day or whenever there is a need to. Being able to clean your pet's enclosure will not only benefit your pet but you and your family as well. Through this process, you'll avoid being infected with diseases which you may get from the fecal matters of your snake. This will not only maintain cleanliness but a safe home as well.

Guidelines on How to Clean Your Snake's Enclosure

Reptiles need special care in terms of cleanliness. Keeping you snake's enclosure clean, sanitized, and odor-free is necessary in keeping a safe and healthy home for your pet. Below are some guidelines on how you'll be able to clean your pet's cage properly.

- Before cleaning, there is a need for you to relocate your snake to a temporary cage in order for you to do all the cleaning and sterilizing. Find a suitable temporary place for your snake to stay. Make sure that the holding cage you are going to prepare for your pet is clean, well ventilated, and secure.

- After that, look for materials inside the cage that needs to be cleaned or replaced like the bedding and the water dish

- Assemble a cleaning kit intended for cleaning the enclosure alone. Gather all the materials that you need like rubber gloves, brushes, paper towels, soap or dish washing, buckets, trash bag, disinfectant, spray bottle, tips, goggles, and sponges

- Make sure to unplug all the electrical devices found on the cage including the heating components and lighting like the heat source, tank heater, and the basking lamp. Take away the thermometer and the gauges too.

- Remove all the furniture items found inside the cage like the water bowls, rocks, branches, climbs, etc. Place them in the sink or bathtub where you are going to wash them.

- Remove the old bedding from the cage. If the substrate is made from aspen shavings or newspaper this process will be easy. You may use a shop vac or you may dump the cage in order to get rid of the substrate. Replace the bedding with a fresh one.

- After emptying the cage, clean it thoroughly. You may use a spray bottle with water and paper towels in order to remove feces, dust, and other dirt. Do not spray cold water over a hot glass or else it might crack. Wait for the cage to cool down before doing so. Use an antibacterial disinfectant afterwards in order to ensure the sanitation of the cage.

- Let the enclosure dry out. Leave it wide open so that the air can dry it completely. You may use a cloth to wipe the glass dry.

- While the cage is being dried, you may now start cleaning the other materials found in the cage, Use a hot water and an antibacterial soap. If the items are really filthy, you may soak the cage furniture in a diluted bleach solution overnight. Use a ratio of 1:4 for bleach and water. Do not scrub the items hard as it may cause scratches and abrasions that would make it harder to clean in the future.

- Be mindful that you must be able to clean the water bowl properly with the use of a "finger scrub". Use a hot water and an antibacterial soap. Scrub it twice and rinse it with the hottest water possible.

- Check if the cage has finished drying. If so, it's time to set it up again. Place the new bedding inside the cage along with all the cage furniture you have cleaned and fill up the water dish with water.

- Plug all the electrical heating device and put back your snake inside the enclosure

- Ensure that all the locks and latches are properly secured.

Husbandry Tips

- Make sure that your snake's enclosure will bring comfort to your pet. Ensure that it has everything it needs like the water bowls, substrate, hiding place, heating equipment, etc.

- When you are feeding your snake, make sure that he is alone to avoid aggression if ever you have other snake pets.

- As much as possible, stay away from your pet until the lump in his body has disappeared. Let it digest the food and absorb all the nutrients it needs before you handle them.

- Make sure that your snake has an access to fresh water. Use a water clean water dish and regularly check if the water is enough for your pet. If you feel like your snake is starting to feel moist, remove the water bowl and return it occasionally.

- Hognose snakes are wild animals in nature so make sure that you handle them carefully and gently. Stay away from holding its head especially on the first days when it still not socialized with its new owner.

- Snakes do shed their old skin so expect that it's going to happen. Do not handle them if they are in the process of shedding. Wait until they already finished getting rid of their old skin before doing so.

- Make sure that your snake will not feel threatened so avoid restraining them. Do not squeeze their body hard. Handle them gently through your fingers and hands.

Illnesses Caused by Unsanitary Living Condition

There are lots of factors that affect the health of your pet and one of it is the living condition. If your pet is living in an unsanitary place there is a tendency that it will catch illnesses or infections.

Dirty places are where mites love to hide. It may eventually go and infect your snake. Watch out for mites especially around your pet's eyes, mouth, and under its scales. Inspect their body if it seems lethargic and losing its appetite. Unsanitary enclosures may cause your snake wheezing that might actually become a respiratory infection. Consult your veterinarian if this happens.

It is necessary for you to have a veterinarian who is a snake expert. It might be hard for you to find a vet that specializes with snake but it is advisable that you'll be able to get connected with this kind of veterinarian. By this, you'll make sure that your snake's health wouldn't be compromised.

Chapter Seven: Dealing and Handling Your Hognose Snakes

Hognose snakes are generally docile and easy to deal with regards to handling and feeding them but sometimes it might become a challenge especially if you have just started socializing your pet with you as its new owner and with everything in his environment that has changed since you brought him home. Though they are found to become well-adjusted easily, still you must be there for them during the process.

In this chapter, you'll be able to learn how to handle Hognose snakes properly, tips on how to feed, handle and tame them.

Dealing with Your Hognose Snake

Adjustment Period

The period of adjustment is the most crucial part. It is the time you let your snake get used to the new environment it belongs to. Although this type of snake has a low disposition and can adjust easily, it still needs your presence in order to overcome this stage.

In the start your snake might feel a little threatened and if it hides or defend themselves, do not worry. It is normal that they will feel aloof at first. Wait for them to fully adjust with the changes it is going through

Familiarizing Yourself

Let your snake stay outside its enclosure for at least an hour each day in order to make your smell familiar to it. Do this as soon as your pet arrives in your home for the first week of its stay. Take caution and it is advisable for you not to touch your Hognose snake on the first few days. Give your Hognose snake a few weeks and let it settle down first on its new habitat.

Feeding Schedule

Set up a regular feeding routine for your new pet. Let it know when it's going to expect meals. By this way, he'll adjust more easily on the new things it will be dealing with.

Probationary Period

Do not stress your pet with unnecessary handling especially on the first few weeks of its stay. It may take some time before your pet will get use to you. On the end of your first week together, you can begin to arrange the things inside your snake's cage but it is still not advisable for you to touch it. Do this for at least one more week to ensure your snake that you are not a threat and won't do any harm. Expose yourself with your pet but make sure that you won't touch it until the right time comes.

After the probationary period, once your snake has already felt safe with your presence, you may now start to touch it gently, move it around the cage, and lift its tail. Do this manner for three to four days.

Handling

If it seems that your pet has already adjusted with the new space it has, you may now start further exposing yourself to it through short periods of handling. Remember not to handle it shortly after a meal. Wait for at least two to three days. When you are approaching your pet, handle it to the side as a predator would approach it to the top. Make sure that you are gentle so that it will not feel any signs of threat.

Supervision

You may ask the supervision of a long-time snake owner or professional in order for you to become comfortable in

Taming Your Hognose Snake

Although Hognose snakes are not that aggressive compared to other types of snakes, there is still a need for you to tame it especially if you had when it's already an adult wherein it doesn't know your smell and wouldn't recognize you as for the reason that the snake didn't grow up under your shelter.

Know the reason why it seems aggressive

You'll likely need to deprogram the aggression your snake is showing and the first thing you have to do is to learn where these aggressive responses are coming from.

Territorial or Defensive Responses

This is actually not an indicator of aggression but these are instinctive responses. Most of their lives, snakes lived in an environment on which they must defend themselves from being eaten by predators. This mechanism can easily be tamed with the help of consistent gentle care.

Feeding Responses

This type of response is just another instinctive response that is natural for snakes to have. Snakes do assume that everything that enters their enclosure is food. Though they less likely to bite its owner, if they thought that you are going to feed it it might strike your hand.

Tips How to Handle and Tame Your Snake

- If your snake is being aggressive, which less likely for a Hognose snake to be, it may require more training for you to tame it and one technique is through the use of hook training. It is done by rubbing its body gently or pushing down it with a hook before you take them out of the cage. By this process, your snake will know that it's not feeding time yet and there is no need for it to bite.

- Snakes can get terrified every time you open their enclosure especially if they aren't socialized well yet. You may also use the hook in order to rub its body and calm it down. When your pet flatten its body, coils into a ball, or pose a position that looks like it's going to strike, just gently rub its body with the use of the hook until it relaxes. Do not start with rubbing the snake's head or else it will feel more threatened and become more frightened. Rub its body down from the end of its tail.

- In order to reprogram the aggression from a feeding response of snake, you may stop feeding your snake every week and feed it once every three weeks and help it get used to you by handling it every day. This will stoop the idea of your pet that everything that comes into its cage is food. It is recommended that you feed your snake in a separate tank to transfer the response from the enclosure to its new feeding area.

- Wash your hands thoroughly before handling your snake. This kind of reptile has an exceptional sensory organ. If they smell a scent of prey on your hand, it might think that it is food. Doing so, will help prevent any germs and bacteria that might infect your pet

- Learn the proper way you should handle your snake on which you'll be able to pick it up properly and handle it without putting strain on its body. Keep support on the first third of your snake's body with either one of your hands or a hook. Give a lightly press on your Hognose snake's head so that it will know it's not time for it to be fed. Do not grab its tail when you are picking it up for this may cause fear and serious strain to your snake.

- If you are new in handling snakes, it might be a little scary handling them especially its head. If you are not yet used to it, you may hold it with its face away from you. Through this you'll be able to expose your snake with the motion of your hands without risking yourself to get bitten.

- Never restrict your snake's head as it may think that you are trying to hurt it or that you are a predator. Just hold its body gently and avoid restraining its head.

- Snakes can be more aggressive during shedding. Avoid handling them when they are under the process of shedding. Wait until their old skin comes off.

Chapter Eight: Breeding Your Hognose Snakes

After gaining knowledge on how to properly handle your snake it's now time for you to learn all about breeding a Hognose snake. If you are planning to expand the snake community you have, this chapter will be of great help for you as it will provide necessary information on how you'll be able to identify the sex of your pet snake, set up a condition for breeding. In this chapter you'll be provided with information about how to identify the sex of your snake along with breeding basics like how to set up an appropriate breeding condition for your pet as well as information on its ovulation, incubation and hatching process.

Sexual Dimorphism

How to determine if your snake is a male or female?

Observation

In general, males are more active than females. You may try to observe their behavior as their sex can be established on the way they move. But still the best way to determine if your snake is a male or female is through the structure of its body. A male's tail is bulbous and a lot more parallel compared to a female's whose tail's shape is tapered. A hemipenes can also be observed whenever your snake is defecating. When your pets do its own thing through a hemipenes it means that it is a male. During shedding, this part of the body becomes more noticeable characterized by a pair of bits of skin which is usually dry found at its vent

Cloacal Popping

One method you may use in order to check the sex of your pet is through the method of "popping". It is done by placing the thumb and pulling the anal scale of the snake that is going to be sexed forward in order to expose and open the vent slightly. The other thumb will squeeze on the underside of the tail using a rocking motion putting the pressure gently on the vent that will cause the male's hemipenes to pop out. Hemipenes are little reddish or pinkish rods that pop outs on the sides of the cloacal opening. A female may response in the pressure by erecting her scent gland papillae which resembles that of the male's hemipenes but it is way smaller and there are no blood vessels visible.

Cloacal Probing

In order to determine the gender of your pet, you may use a slender probe by pushing it on the cloaca's posterior wall in order to see if it can be pushed gently and freely in the tail's base. This technique has been introduced by Blanchard and Finster in the year 1933. Make sure that you are using an appropriate size of probe. How far the probe goes is the way to determine its sex. Approximately, the probe will slide for 10 scales if it's a male and goes for 3 to 4 scales if it's a female. If the probe goes between these ranges the snake can be classified as unsexed. You may ask for your veterinarian's assistance especially if you have no experience with sexing snakes.

How to Set Up the Right Breeding Conditions

Breeding snakes seems complicated but actually it is pretty easy. All you need to do is to know all the preparation you have to do in order to have a successful breeding. It is vital for your snake to feel that its breeding environment is similar with that of the wild on which they usually breed depending on the situation or season. If it feels like it's not yet the proper time to reproduce, it might be hard for you to breed your snake.

Below are the things you have to consider in order to prepare your pet for its reproduction.

- **Set the Mood**

The interest of snakes to breed is usually based on the urge, photoperiod, and temperature. Typically, snakes are sexually active during the cold months of the winter season. This factor should really not be compromised as it is very important for the snake's instinct to breed. You must be able to provide a cooler temperature as well as longer nights for your pet snake. The temperature during daytime should range 77 to 84 degrees Fahrenheit and 69 to 73 Fahrenheit during night-time and these cool temperatures should last for 2 to 3 months. There should also be at least 12 hours of darkness. You may set up this condition through controlling the enclosure's temperature and by putting it in a place on which you can easily dim the room. At the end of the winter season, you may now slowly increase the temperature and resume to a normal one.

- **Check for Signs of Follicle Growth**

    Examine the part of your snake's body near its gallbladder and look for follicle growth. Feel the bumps on its body that may be found about 2/3 down its body and try to measure it through slightly pinching your fingers in it. Let its body run through your fingers to make this process easier. If you want to have an accurate measurement, you may also bring your pet to its veterinarian and let it undergo an ultrasound procedure to see if its follicles are growing. If the follicle of your pet snake reaches 10 to 12 millimetres it indicates that your snake is in a good point to start breeding.

- **Stimulate Courtship for Copulation**

    After setting up the correct breeding condition and determining and hitting the right number and measurement of follicle growth, it is now time to introduce both the male and female snake to each other. An ideal pair should goes like this;. The females should be bigger and heavier than males so that they'll be able to handle the male's body weight without stressing the process of egg production. Usually, females are paired when they reach the age of 3 or 4 years old. On the other hand, males are being paired younger than females. When they reach their ideal weight they are immediately paired. The breeding pair should be in the best state of health.

You may observe jerky movements from the start. They usually follow each other around the enclosure. The male will flick its tongue on the female's body and will rub its chin on her back. Observe the two snakes carefully. If the female raises and wiggles its tail it means that she is properly responding and ready to breed. The male will twist his tail under the tail of the female's attempting to start the mating. It may take several hours and you can do this process for 3 to 5 times for a better chance of reproduction. You may use the three day rule on which you will let the two snakes together in the cage for 3 days and let them apart or 3 days and repeat.

- **Feed your snake with the right range of food**

During copulation, your female snake will start to go off of food especially when its follicles reach 20 to 22 mm. There is a need for you to give them more food. Feed your female snake as much as she could at least more than her normal range towards food.

Ovulation and Laying

After copulation, the female will start to ovulate and will store the sperm eggs into its oviduct afterwards in the span of 2 months in order to get it fertilized. The gestation period for Hognose snakes lasts for 28 to 45 days and it is important for you to provide it with a meal twice a week. If it refuses to eat, do not worry since it only means that for at least 2 weeks she is going to lay eggs. Make sure that the substrate of your snake is damp and not wet. Before the process of egg-laying occurs, a pre-egg laying shed precedes for 7 to 12 days before oviposition.

Set up a nesting box for your pet. It can be made from a plastic container filled with moss. Make sure it has a secure lid with holes on the top. Make sure that the size of the nesting box is appropriate for your pet. Consider the factors such as its age, size, and the size of the eggs as well. The size of the clutches can be from 8 to 25 or more eggs.

Incubation and Hatching of Eggs

After the eggs have been laid, transfer them from the nesting box to an incubation container filled with moistened vermiculite. Punch holes in the side of the container instead in the lid. Put the container inside an incubator with a temperature of 78 to 84 degrees. Check on it from time to time but do not disturb it. Usually, hatching occurs after 48 to 60 days of incubation which may vary depending on the temperature of the incubator. If the eggs are small, yellow in color, waxy or with a wet appearance, and/or misshapen, it might indicate that it is a bad egg. If ever you encounter a bad egg, put them in a separate container.

The moment that the neonates emerge from their eggs, do not bother them. Once they have absorbed the yolk they will fully leave their eggs. Transfer the baby snakes in a container made of plastic with proper ventilation, damp paper towels, and a water dish. They should stay together until they first shed their skin. Their first meal can be offered 7 to 10 days after they hatch or after they shed their skin.

How to Become a Successful and Reputable Breeder

If you have the desire to become a reputable breeder someday, make sure that you are ready to commit your time, effort, and care for your snake especially during this phase. Do not just breed for them for the sake of breeding but make sure that you are able to consider many factors mentioned a while ago. You must not stress out your snake just because you want them to produce more eggs. The health and happiness of your pet should never be compromised. If you follow all these tips, you'll surely become a successful snake breeder.

Chapter Nine: Common Diseases and Treatments for Hognose Snakes

Although snakes are powerful reptiles, they aren't that prone to different diseases. Snakes do not usually get ill but still they have the tendency to catch diseases especially if they are exposed to a not so good environmental condition. As they say, prevention is better than cure. With proper care and nutrition, you'll be able to help it avoid developing any sickness. Always observe you pet. If it seems lethargic and doesn't eat well, bring it to the vet immediately to check if it is sick.

In this chapter, you'll be able to know the common ailments of Hognose snakes and the treatments your snake may undergo in order to get well.

Common Health Problems

In this segment, you'll be able to discover some of the most common health problems a Hognose snake might potentially face. Watch out for their signs and symptoms as it can help save their lives and save you bucks as well.

Parasites

External Parasites

Wild-caught snakes are the ones who usually have mites and ticks. On the contrary, a captive bred is likely to have these parasites on the skin. Having external parasites is very common for Hognose snakes. Mites and ticks are somehow similar to each other. They suck the blood of its host or your snake for instance and they usually come in great numbers. They will look like tiny black balloons protruding from your pet's skin.

There are two ways for your snake to have external parasites: Through the wild and through direct contact with a snake that has already ticks on their skin

Treatment:

You may use a pair of tweezers in order to remove these parasites from your snake's body. You may use a powder or spray specially formulated for snakes intended to kill ticks and mites. Make sure to clean and sanitize your pet's cage. Soak it using water and bleach and clean it thoroughly. Keep the cleanliness of your snake's enclosure to avoid these parasites from coming.

Internal Parasites

Hognose snakes can have parasites within their bloodstream, inside their bodies, and in their organs like the in their intestines. Worms, nematodes, and flukes are some of just the internal parasites that might live inside your pet's body. These kinds of parasites are harder to detect as they are not seen and obvious through the use of the naked eye. These ailments may be caused by stressful periods like

injuries. If your snake is losing weight, losing appetite, and if
it has blood in its stools, your pet might have internal
parasites. If you have seen these symptoms bring your snake
to the veterinarian immediately.

Treatment:

Internal Parasites can be detected through a fecal
examination. It is important for you to bring your pet to
your veterinarian in order to attend to this illness. Make sure
that you are feeding high-quality food to your snake and
keep it healthy in order to avoid these kind of parasites.

Dehydration

If it seems like your snake is having trouble on
shedding its skin, it could be a sign that your pet is
dehydrated.

Treatment:

Water is the best defense against dehydration and all
the problems that might follow. Make sure that your snake
has access to fresh water at all times. Check the level of

humidity of the enclosure where your snake is located. Create a moisture retreat for your pet especially if you live in a dry place with low-humidity.

Dysecdysis

This ailment is a problem with regard to shedding of the skin. This may be caused by dehydration and the presence of external parasites. This is not a disease but a symptom of a disease. As soon as the snake completed its skin shedding, a new cycle will begin. The length of the shedding cycle depends on your pet's nutritional state and age. A healthy snake is expected to undergo shedding a least once a month. Every time your snake shed, check that the eye caps or spectacles do come off along with the shed. If ever it gets stuck or retained an infection might occur.

Treatment:

Soak your pet by putting it in a moisture box or by putting a damp pillow case on its enclosure. After an hour or so, try to pull off the retained skin as much as possible. You must be able to duplicate the motion of it is supposed to come off. Use a warm washcloth and gently rub it on you pet's skin in order to further remove the old skin. You may do this process for 2 to 3 times. This will help soften the stubborn shed helping your snake be able to get rid of it all by itself.

Vomiting and Regurgitation

Regurgitation is the casting up of undigested food inside your snake's body or stomach. Poor husbandry is said to be the major cause of this ailment. It is defined by waves of contraction that are mild and moving backwards up the body of your pet.

On the other hand, vomiting is characterized by a forceful ejection of food inside the small intestine or stomach. The vomit will often look like feces with no urates. This is usually caused by intestinal parasite infections, intestinal obstructions, and bacterial infections.

Treatment:

Fasting might be recommended by your veterinarian while you are waiting for the medications to take effect. After such period, your snake might be advised to be tube fed since liquid meals are easier to digest. This might be needed to be done for a few days before your pet will be allowed on its regular diet.

To avoid dehydration from regurgitating or vomiting, your snake might be administered with fluid therapy through the subcutaneous or intraperitoneal fluids.

These types of fluids cannot be taken orally as your snake might just vomit it again. Drug therapy is another way to treat this condition. Amoebic infections and nematode should be treated with de-wormers or anti-parasite drugs while bacterial infections require antibiotics.

If your snake has been diagnosed with obstruction, it might undergo surgery or endoscopy in order to take away the blockage since it might interfere with the blood circulation to the wall of the intestines.

Infectious Stomatitis (Mouth Rot)

This condition affects both the teeth and gums. It is a consequence of stress, poor husbandry, and inadequate nutrition. It is characterized by a mouth infection

Treatment:

Medical procedures such as x-rays, bacterial cultures, blood tests, and laboratory testing are necessary in order to properly diagnose this illness.

Pneumonia

This is a common respiratory problem for snakes. This involves the airways, the lungs, or the nasal cavity. Respiratory diseases come from stuffy nose to fulminate pneumonia. A sign for this ailment is a nasal discharge. Pneumonia for reptiles is a very fatal disease. Snakes don't have any diaphragm and as a result their lungs are being filled with pus and they may have a difficulty when it comes to breathing. Snakes with pneumonia often prop themselves with its head and neck held high and its mouth wide open.

Treatment:

Antibiotics might be needed to be administered in order to get rid of the infection. X-rays, cytology, pulmonary washes, bacterial culture, and sensitivity testing might be needed. If the case is already advanced, CT, endoscopy, or MRI are some of the procedures that may be needed. This is a serious disease therefore is in need of proper medical attention.

Chapter Nine: Common Diseases and Treatments for Hognose Snakes

Chapter Ten: Care Sheet and Summary

The last and definitely not the least chapter! After learning all the essentials of Hognose snake care, we'll give you a synopsis of all the important factors tackled in the previous chapters. If ever you are in a hurry, a quick glance will be enough for you to be able to review the things you need to know without the need to go over the whole book again. We hope that this book has helped you in more ways than you have expected. We hope that you continue to gain more knowledge on how you'll be able to become a responsible owner and breeder. Learning never stops. We hope you'll continue to seek more ways on how you'll be able to take care of your Hognose snake.

Biological Information

Taxonomy: They belong in Kingdom *Animalia*, Phylum *Chordata*, Class *Reptilia*, Order *Squamata*, Family *Dipsadidae*, Genus *Heterodon*, and Species *nasicus/ simus/ platyrhinos*

Country of Origin: North America, South America, Madagascar, Dry and sandy lands

Size: 24 inches to 84 inches

Body Type and Appearance: It has a stout body covered with keeled scales and it has an upturned snout.

Color: Its ground color comes in a variety ranging from brown, gray or olive, tan, and somewhat has dark blotches with a square or bar shape that runs along its body longitudinally. It has black scales that are glossy. Its scales can often be white, orange, or yellow.

Defense Mechanism: If threatened, it has the capacity to flatten its body that might be an attempt to make itself look dangerous and larger that would sent the predator away. It might also strike but usually with a closed mouth either forward or sideways to knock its predator down with the use of its keeled snout without the need of biting.

Sub – Species of Hognose Snakes:

Heterodon Nasicus - Western Hognose: Its ground color comes in a variety ranging from brown, gray or olive, tan, and somewhat has dark blotches with a square or bar shape that runs along its body longitudinally

Heteredon Simus- Southern Hognose Snake: They come in colors tan, gray, or reddish with a hint of dark brown blotches at the center of its back and along the sides.

Heterodon Platyrhinos- Eastern Hognose: Their body background can be gray, black, brown, yellow, green.

Lifespan: 15 years to 18 years

Hognose Snakes as Pets

Temperament: Hognose Snakes are unlikely to be hostile making them easy to be managed. Although they are part of the wild, their aggression is at the lowest level. Snakes often bite but not Hognose Snakes. They rarely try to bite owners as even in the most threatened circumstance they might strike with their mouths closed or they might even play dead. They get easily accustomed to the new environment they belong to. Their low disposition can be maintained especially if they are properly socialized.

Other pets: Their temperament toward other pets is just the same unless they are toads and rodents since these two are their main prey. They can get along well with other animals as long as they have been properly socialized with each other. But it is still best for you not to associate them with other animals.

Major Pro: They are non-venomous. They are unlikely to use biting as a defense mechanism. Instead, they rely on bluffing ploys like playing dead in order to escape extreme situations. When they are threatened, they may strike but with their mouths closed. They really have a low disposition which is a great factor since aggression is not a problem.

Major Con: This pet is definitely not for those who have a faint heart as living with a snake can really make you feel unusual unless you are strong-willed to really keep one. It cannot also be trained though it can be socialized. You cannot expect so much from this pet, unlike dogs who can express what their feel through their body language. The food it needs might only be purchased on pet shops or reptile stores. They can live for 15 years which is a downside as it may be hard to rehome.

Legal Requirements and Snake Licensing:

Hognose Snakes need not to be licensed since they are categorized as non-venomous meaning that even if their bite won't kill anyone as the venom they have won't harm human unless they are allergic to it. But still it depends on which state or country you belong. There might not be a mandatory requirement for licensing but permits might be regulated. Make sure that you are familiar with all the laws or ordinance in the place you live in with regard to snake licensing.

Necessary documents needed (may vary)

- Owner's identification documents

- Pet Insurance

- Medical History

- Micro-chipping

- Medical Certificates

- Other proofs showing that you have bought your snake from a recognized breeder who breed them in captivity and not just caught in the wild.

Habitat Requirements for Hognose Snakes: Enclosure, substrate, heating,, hiding place, separate food tank

Purchasing and Selecting a Healthy Breed

Where to Purchase: Reptile Shops, Private Breeders, Reptile Shows, Rescue Centers

Characteristics of a Reputable Breeder:

- They should be knowledgeable enough about the breed/ specie of snake they are raising. They must be able to provide you information on how this breed behave and how it should properly be taken care of

- They should be able to provide you other information that aren't typical. They should know more than a pet store clerk. If they only provide you with details that are general, there's a big chance that they aren't really pet enthusiasts.

- Reputable breeders should be able to build a good relationship with their potential/ existing buyers

- Good Breeders have lots of patience especially to those who keep on asking questions. They have the initiative to share what they know without getting frustrated or angry with them.

- They should ask questions about you as they are making sure that you are responsible enough to handle whichever pet you have chosen. This is actually a good sign that the breeder care about pets

Characteristics of a Healthy Breed: The eyes should be free from any sign of discharge or cloudiness. There should be no signs of discharge in the nostrils and that it's free from any signs of labor breathing. The body of the snake should be rounded without any injuries. If the snake has a smooth and supple skin or if has blisters do not purchase it as these are signs of ill health. It should also have no mobility issues and should have the capacity to move freely.

Habitat Requirements for Hognose Snakes:

How to Set Up Habitat for Your Snake:

Step 1: Find the right size tank

Step 2: Decide where you are going to place the heating paraphernalia

Step 3: Add the substrate/ bedding of your choice

Step 4: Add the necessary accessories inside the cage

Step 5: Install all the heating equipment

Nutritional Requirements

In the wild: In the wild, Hognose snakes being their carnivorous selves would feed on toads, birds, and small mammals.

In captivity: When they are already held captive the diet you'll be able to provide for them will of course be limited. The best food you can give them is domesticated rodents which are already frozen and easy to stock in your freezer, though there is still a need for you to warm it before serving it to your pet.

Feeding Conditions: In order to encourage your snake to eat, you must make sure that nothing's going to bother it. During feeding time, your snake should be away from any factors that might cause them to lose their appetite.

Feeding Amount/Frequency: Hognose snakes have a high metabolism rate. They need to be fed a minimum of twice per week. The recommended size of a snake's meal should not be bigger than the width of the its body or the size of the meal should only leave a small lump in its body.

How to Feed Hognose Snake:

- After feeding your Hognose snake, do not handle it for at least 24 hours. Let it digest the food first for it to absorb all the nutrients it needs. It is not ideal for you to handle them right away so avoid doing so.

- Make sure that your snake has access to fresh water. Remember to check if the dish has enough water for your pet and constantly replenish them with it.
- Do not force them to eat when they refuse to.
- Do not serve frozen pre-killed prey. Instead, place it inside a plastic bag and thaw it under running warm water.
- Make sure that you are able to feed your pet with the correct size of meal they need.
- Use thongs in feeding your snake

Maintenance for Hognose Snakes

Spot Cleaning Your Snake's Enclosure:

It is recommended that you clean your snake's cage at least once a day, or every other day or whenever there is a need to. Being able to clean your pet's enclosure will not only benefit it but you and your family as well. Through this process, you'll avoid being infected with diseases which you may get from the fecal matters of your pet. This will not only maintain cleanliness but a healthy home as well.

Guidelines on How to Clean Your Snake's Enclosure

- Before cleaning, there is a need for you to relocate your snake to a temporary cage in order for you to do all the cleaning and sterilizing. Find a suitable temporary place for your snake to stay.

- After that, look for materials inside the cage that needs to be cleaned or replaced like the bedding and the water dish.

- Assemble a cleaning kit intended for cleaning the enclosure alone. Gather all the materials that you need like rubber gloves, brushes, paper towels, soap or dish washing, buckets, trash bag, disinfectant, spray bottle, q-tips, goggles, and sponges.

- Make sure to unplug all the electrical devices found on the cage.

- Remove all the furniture items found inside the cage like the water bowls, rocks, branches, climbs, etc.

- Remove the old bedding from the cage.

- After emptying the cage, clean it thoroughly. You may use a spray bottle with water and paper towels in order to remove feces, dust, and other dirt.

- Let the enclosure dry out.

- While the cage is being dried, you may now start cleaning the other materials found in the cage. Use a hot water and an antibacterial soap.

- Be mindful that you must be able to clean the water bowl properly with the use of a "finger scrub".

- Check if the cage has finished drying. If so, it's time to set it up again. Place the new bedding inside the cage along with all the cage furniture you have cleaned and fill up the water bowl with water.

- Plug all the electrical heating device and put back your snake inside the enclosure.

- Ensure that all the locks and latches are properly secured.

Dealing and Handling Your Hognose Snakes

- **Adjustment Period -** It is the time you let your snake get used to the new it belongs to. Although this type of snake has a low disposition and can adjust easily, it still need your presence in order to overcome this stage.

- **Familiarizing yourself -** Let your snake stay outside its enclosure for at least an hour each day it in order to make your smell familiar. Do this as soon as your pet arrives in your home for the first week of its stay.

- **Feeding Schedule-** Set up a regular feeding routine for your new pet. Let it know when it's going to expect meals.
- **Probationary Period-**On the end of your first week together, you can begin to arrange the things inside your snake's cage but it is still not advisable for you to touch it.
- **Handling-** If it seems that your pet has already adjusted with the new space it has, you may now start further exposing yourself to it through short periods of handling.
- **Supervision-** You may ask the supervision of a long-time snake owner or professional in order for you to become comfortable in

Taming Your Snake

- You'll likely need to deprogram the aggression your snake is showing and the first thing you have to do is to learn where these aggressive responses are coming from.

  Territorial or Defensive Responses -This is actually not an indicator of aggression but these are instinctive responses. Most of their lives, snakes lived in an environment on which they must defend themselves from being eaten by predators.

Feeding Responses - This type of response is just another instinctive response; Snakes do assume that everything that enters their enclosure is food. Though they less likely to bite its owner, if they thought that you are going to feed it might strike your hand.

Breeding Your Hognose Snakes

Sexual Dimorphism:

In general, males are more active than females. You may try to observe their behaviour as their sex can be established on the way they move. But still the best way to determine if your snake is a male or female is through the structure of its body. A male's tail is bulbous and a lot more parallel compared to a female's whose tail's shape is tapered. A hemi-penis can also be observed whenever your snake is defecating.

How to Set Up the Right Breeding Conditions:

• **Set the Mood**

Typically, snakes are sexually active during the cold months of the winter season. The temperature during daytime should range 77 to 84 degrees Fahrenheit and 69 to 73 Fahrenheit during night-time and these cool temperatures should last for 2 to 3 months. There should also be at least 12 hours of darkness. You may set up this condition through controlling the enclosure's temperature and by putting it in a place on which you can easily dim the room.

- **Check for Signs of Follicle Growth**

Examine the part of your snake's body near its gallbladder and look for follicle growth. Feel the bumps on its body that may be found about 2/3 down its body and try to measure it through slightly pinching your fingers in it. If the follicle of your pet snake reaches 10 to 12 millimetres it indicates that your snake is in a good point to start breeding.

- **Stimulate Courtship for Copulation**

An ideal pair should goes like this;. The females should be bigger and heavier than males so that they'll be able to handle the male's body weight without stressing the process of egg production. You may observe jerky movements from the start. They usually follow each other around the enclosure. The male will flick its tongue on the female's body and will rub its chin on her back. It may take several hours and you can do this process for 3 to 5 times for a better chance of reproduction. You may use the three day rule on which you will let the two snakes together in the cage for 3 days and let them apart or 3 days and repeat.

- **Feed your snake with the right range of food**

    During copulation, your female snake will start to go off of food especially when its follicles reach 20 to 22 mm. There is a need for you to give them more food. Feed your female snake as much as she could at least more than her normal range towards food.

Sexual Maturity: 3-4 years

Incubation Period: Usually, hatching occurs after 48 to 60 days of incubation which may vary depending on the temperature of the incubator.

Litter Size: The size of the clutches can be from 8 to 25 or more eggs

Common Diseases and Health Requirements

Parasites (External and Internal), Dehydration, Dysecdysis, Vomiting and Regurgitation, Infectious Stomatitis (Mouth Rot), and Pneumonia.

Glossary of Snake Terms

1.2.3 - helps to denote how many species does a person own including the sex of the animals. 1 is for the male, 2 for female, and 3 for unknown.

Amel- a short term for amelanistic which is a term used to define a reptile with no colors black and brown in its skin

Amplexus- scientific term used to define the sexual coupling of Anurans. During this process, the male tightly graps onto the female from behind in order to achieve fertilization

Anery-a term which refers to any reptile without any red colouration in the skin. A short term for aneythristic.

Aquatic- a specie dwelling the water

Arboreal- a specie dwelling in the trees. Most of the time they spend off the ground. They are also considered as climbing species

BCI- Boa Constrictor imperator abbreviation

BCC- Boa constrictor constrictor

Brumation- hibernation of reptiles

Carapace- upper domed shell found on turtles, terrapins, crustaceans, and tortoise

CB- it means Captive Breed

Chelonian- describes turtles, tortoises, and terrapins collectively

CITES- Convention on International Trade in Endangered Species. An agreement regulating thousands of endangered animals and plants, controlling their importation and exportation

Cloaca- term for vent

Crepuscular- dawn and dusk; active during twilight

Diurnal- active during the day

DWA- Dangerous Wild Animals Act

Ectothermic- means cold blooded.

Estivation- it is when dormancy occurs during dry or hot seasons in order to escape the heat or remain hydrated

Faunarium- fitted enclosure made of plastic with air-holed lid

FK- Fresh Killed

Flexarium- enclosure for reptiles

Fossorial- species that are fond or burrowing and spends a lot of time underground

Fuzzy- a rodent whose size reached the "fur growing "stage of development

F/T- froze/thawed

Gravid- a pregnant reptile

Gut-loading- the process of feeding insects with nutritious food 24 hours before becoming a prey item and be fed to your pet.

Hatchling- a baby reptile that is newly hatched

Hemipenes- defined by two/ dual sex organs

Herbivorous- animals that only eat on plants such as vegetables, flowers, and leaves.

Herps/Herpetiles- covers all species of amphibian and repltile collectively

Herpetoculturist- a person who takes care of captive reptiles

Herpetology- the study of Amphibians and Reptiles

Het- heterozygous- a reptile that carries a recessive gene for a morph

Hide Box- gives the snake a secure place

Hots- snakes that are venomous

Husbandry- - it describes an animal's every day care

Hygrometer- a tool used for measuring humidity

Impaction- defined by a blockage in the digestive tract

Incubate- maintain the egs in a favorable condition for development and hatching

Interstitial- skin between scales

Insectivorous- animals that eat on insects

Juvenile- an animal that is sub-adult or not quite an adult for breeding

Larvae- plural form of larva; insects or amphibians facing the stage of pre-metamorphosis

Leucistic- an animal with dark eyes

LTC- Long Term Captive

MBD- Metabolic Bone Disease

Metamorphosis- a process of change

Musking- defensive ploy of snakes wherein they secrete a small amount of foul smelling liquid coming from its vent whenever agitated or frightened.

Omnivorous- animals that may eat on both meat and plants

Oviparous- female that lay eggs

Ovoviviparous- eggs that are developing stays inside the female's body until hatching

Pinkie- newborn/ baby rodent

PK- Pre-killed

Popping- a procedure made in order to determine the sec of the hatchlings

---

Probing- it where a prone is going to be inserted in the snake's vent in order to determine its sex

Pip- act of hatching a snake by the use of a special tooth

Regurge- a term used short for regurgation; a disease of reptiles caused by poor habitat conditions

RUB- Really Useful Box

Shake & Bake- a slang that denotes a method of coating a feeder insect with vitamin powder and calcium before feeding to your pet

Sloughing- shedding

Sub-Adult- not fully grown reptiles; resemble and adult but not yet ready for breeding

Substrate- a bedding that lines the bottom of a reptile's or amphibian's enclosure

Stat- short term for thermostat

Tag/Tagged- term used for being bitten or for a bite

Terrarium- type of an enclosure for a reptile

Terrestrial- animals that live on the ground

Thermo- regulation- the ability of cold-blooded animals to control their own body temperature

Vent- term used to define a reptile's Cloaca

Vivarium (viv)- a glass enclosure for reptiles

Viviparous- gives birth in order to live young

WC- Wild Caught

Weaner- a sub-adult rodent

WF- Wild Farmed

Yearling- a reptile that has reached a year old

Zoonosis- a type of illness that can be passed from animal to man

Index

E

F

G

H

Y

Photo Credits

Page 1 Photo by user Peter Paplanus via Flickr.com,
https://www.flickr.com/photos/2ndpeter/27232938000/

Page 3 Photo by user Eleanor via Flickr.com,
https://www.flickr.com/photos/daughterdragon/8245340405/

Page 11 Photo by user Peter Paplanus via Flickr.com,
https://www.flickr.com/photos/2ndpeter/17130316660/

Page 25 Photo by user lostnjbro via Flickr.com,
https://www.flickr.com/photos/lostnjboro/33198568540/

Page 39 Photo by user Pater Paplanus via Flickr.com,
https://www.flickr.com/photos/2ndpeter/29833441881/

Page 39 Photo by user Teddy Fotiou via Flickr.com,
https://www.flickr.com/photos/epochcatcher/8089413302/

Page 46 Photo by user OZinOH via Flickr.com,
https://www.flickr.com/photos/75905404@N00/4461481741/

Page 52 Photo by user Natalie McNear via Flickr.com,
https://www.flickr.com/photos/midasvanderhand/620607535
4/

Page 70 Photo by user Natalie McNear via Flickr.com, https://www.flickr.com/photos/midasvanderhand/7303863910/

Page 79 Photo by user Jon Fife via Flickr.com, https://www.flickr.com/photos/good-karma/442293972/

Page 87 Photo by user John Fife via Flickr.com, https://www.flickr.com/photos/good-karma/3456018929/

References

"Breeding Snakes" Breedingsnakes.com

<http://breedingsnakes.com/>

"Care and Breeding the Western Hog-nosed Snake" Reptiles Magazine

<http://www.reptilesmagazine.com/Breeding-Snakes/Breeding-Western-Hog-Nosed-Snake/>

"Common Health Problems in Snakes" Reptileknowledge.com

<http://www.reptileknowledge.com/care/snake-health.php />

"Determining the Sex of Snakes" Vpi.com

<http://vpi.com/publications/determining_the_sex_of_snakes/>

"Eastern Hognose Snake" Animalspot.net

<http://www.animalspot.net/eastern-hognose-snake.html />

"Eastern Hognose Snake" Nhptv.org

<http://www.nhptv.org/wild/easternhognosesnake.asp/>

"Hognose Care Sheet" Thehognosesnake.co.uk

<http://www.thehognosesnake.co.uk/hognose_snake_care_s
heet.htm/>

"Hognose Snakes" Britannica.com
<https://www.britannica.com/animal/hognose-snake/>
"Hognose Snakes" Hognose.co.uk

<http://www.hognose.co.uk/Hognose%20care.htm />

"Hognose Snakes" Lihs.org

<http://www.lihs.org/files/caresheets/Heterodon.htm/>

"Hognose Snakes As Pets" Animals.mom.me

<http://animals.mom.me/hog-nose-snakes-pets-2617.html/>

"Hognose Snake Feeding" Reptilesmagazine.com

<http://www.reptilesmagazine.com/Snake-
Care/Feeding%20Hognose-Snakes/>

"How to Clean A Snakes Cage Easily" Reptileknowledge.com

<http://www.reptileknowledge.com/news/how-to-clean-a-snake-cage-quickly-and-easily/>

"Regurgitation (Vomiting) in snakes" Petplace.com

<https://www.petplace.com/article/reptiles/general/regurgitation-vomiting-in-snakes/>

"Snake Health 101" Reptilesmagazine.com

<http://www.reptilesmagazine.com/Snakes/Snake-Health-101/>

"The Captive Care of Hognose Snakes" Reptileknowledge.com

<http://www.rcptileknowledge.com/care/hognose.php />

"The Reptilian Glossary" Thereptilian.co.uk

<http://www.thereptilian.co.uk/the_reptilian_glossary.html />

"Western Hognose Snake Care Sheet" Reptilesmagazine.com

<http://www.reptilesmagazine.com/Western-Hognose-Snake-Care-Sheet/>

"What Makes A Hognose Snake The Perfect Pet For You" Reptilecentre.com

<http://www.reptilecentre.com/blog/2015/03/what-makes-a-hognose-snake-the-perfect-pet-for-you/>

Feeding Baby
Cynthia Cherry
978-1941070000

Axolotl
Lolly Brown
978-0989658430

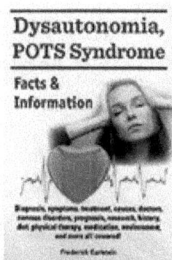

Dysautonomia, POTS
Syndrome
Frederick Earlstein
978-0989658485

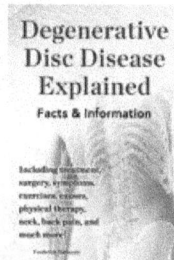

Degenerative Disc
Disease Explained
Frederick Earlstein
978-0989658485

Sinusitis, Hay Fever,
Allergic Rhinitis Explained
Frederick Earlstein
978-1941070024

Wicca
Riley Star
978-1941070130

Zombie Apocalypse
Rex Cutty
978-1941070154

Capybara
Lolly Brown
978-1941070062

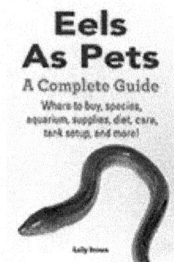

Eels As Pets
Lolly Brown
978-1941070167

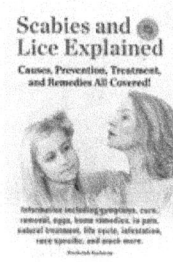

Scabies and Lice Explained
Frederick Earlstein
978-1941070017

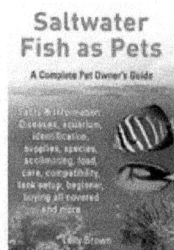

Saltwater Fish As Pets
Lolly Brown
978-0989658461

Torticollis Explained
Frederick Earlstein
978-1941070055

Kennel Cough
Lolly Brown
978-0989658409

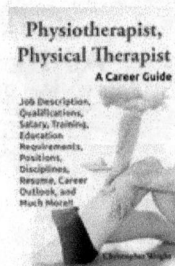

Physiotherapist, Physical
Therapist
Christopher Wright
978-0989658492

Rats, Mice, and Dormice
As Pets
Lolly Brown
978-1941070079

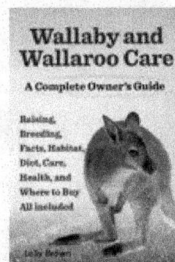

Wallaby and Wallaroo Care
Lolly Brown
978-1941070031

Bodybuilding Supplements
Explained
Jon Shelton
978-1941070239

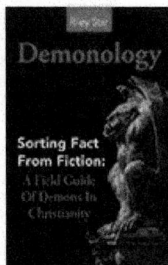

Demonology
Riley Star
978-19401070314

Pigeon Racing
Lolly Brown
978-1941070307

Dwarf Hamster
Lolly Brown
978-1941070390

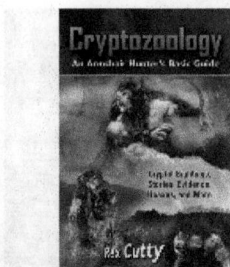

Cryptozoology
Rex Cutty
978-1941070406

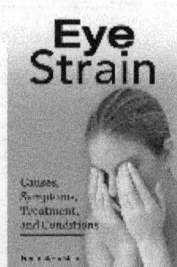

Eye Strain
Frederick Earlstein
978-1941070369

Inez The Miniature Elephant
Asher Ray
978-1941070353

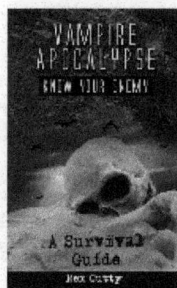

Vampire Apocalypse
Rex Cutty
978-1941070321

www.ingramcontent.com/pod-product-compliance
Lightning Source LLC
Chambersburg PA
CBHW070014110426
42741CB00034B/1731